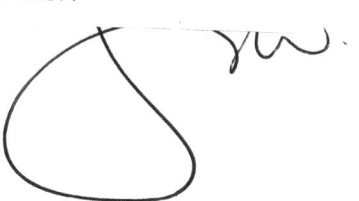

IT'S BEHIND HER
Smile

IT'S BEHIND HER Smile

LATASHA S. WOODCOCK

Tandem Light Press

Tandem Light Press
950 Herrington Rd.
Suite C128
Lawrenceville, GA 30044

Copyright © 2016 by LaTasha Woodcock

All rights reserved. No part of this book may be reproduced, scanned, or transmitted in any printed, electronic, mechanical, including photocopying, recording, or any information storage and retrieval system, without permission in writing from the publisher. Please do not participate in or encourage piracy of copyrighted materials in violation of the author's rights.

Tandem Light Press paperback edition August 2016

ISBN: 978-0-9972296-9-1
Library of Congress Control Number: 2016941736

Biblical passages are from the King James Bible

PRINTED IN THE UNITED STATES OF AMERICA

This book is dedicated and in memory of my grandmother Inez McGee Givens. The time has finally come!

It's Behind Her Smile *is from your faith in God, believing in me and your prayers.*

"Brethren, I count not myself to have apprehended: but this one thing I do, forgetting those things which are behind, and reaching forth unto those things which are before…"

Philippians 3:13

Contents

Foreword	xi
Acknowledgments	xiii
Introduction	xvii
Chapter 1	3
Chapter 2	17
Chapter 3	27
Chapter 4	39
Chapter 5	49
Chapter 6	65
Epilogue	77
In Memorium	81
About the Author	83

Foreword

There is a saying that perfectly describes this book: "you see the glory but don't know the story." Many people see the woman with a beautiful family, two degrees, and a job, but very few know the story.

It wasn't always easy being a child of a single mom. There were many nights when I would go to sleep with my mom there and wake up in the middle of the night to look over and see that she was gone. She wasn't going out to party like you might think, but she was working third shift to make sure I had everything I needed. My mom worked hard trying to make sure that although she was a single parent, my life was as normal as possible.

I was so excited to hear that she was writing a book and all that she had worked hard for was happening. My mom's story is both inspiring and life changing. I never knew everything behind my mother's smile because she didn't want me to worry. To hear all that she's been through and still overcame — it is amazing. Hearing her story has let me know that I can make it through anything.

This story will motivate you to continue to push and strive until you reach your goals. It is not just for the single moms/dads but for everyone that is willing to read it. My mom, Latasha S. Woodcock, had to face many challenges, which you will read about, but she still made it. Everything that we face in life is for a purpose. This story is just confirmation that whatever you're going through or went through was for a reason. If you read this book with an open heart and mind, you will be inspired by this amazing story.

I am so proud of my mom and all that she has accomplished. This book is a dream come true for her. You have seen the glory and now you will know the story. What's behind your smile?

Marquis D. Gore, Son

Acknowledgments

I thank God for allowing me the opportunity to birth my gift that He planted in me. I thank God for showering me with His grace and mercy over the years. I thank God for my husband Howard, my number one supporter, number one fan. My husband has been my encourager, motivator and has strengthened me when I was weak. I thank you honey for allowing me to follow my dream and birth my gift. Thank you for allowing me to miss out on family time, cooking, cleaning, and staying up late at night to get my book done. Thank you for your prayers, love and support, I am who I am today because of who you are to me.

Thank you to my first born, my oldest son Marquis. Thank you for your support, your assistance, your creativity, your encouragement, and your prayers. Thank you to my Babygirl, my Tinkerbell, my only daughter Ny'Zeria. Thank you for being my number one cheerleader and helping me out with any and everything. Thank you to my two youngest sons Eric and Denzil. Thank you both for being supportive, understanding, loving, and helping me out whenever I need you both.

Thank you to my parents George and Patricia for raising me the best way you knew how. Thank you for your love and support. Thank you for being here for me and assisting me so that I could accomplish my dreams. Thank you for your sacrifices and prayers.

Thank you to my siblings, George Jr. (Chandra), Clifton (Renae) for your love, understanding, support, and prayers. Thanks for believing in me and allowing me to be who I am.

Thank you to my spiritual parents: Pastor Elvie and Mother Rutha Jenkins, Sr. Thank you for always praying with and for me. Thank you for your tremendous support over the years. Thank you for your leadership and encouragement. Thank you for believing in me as well as my family. Thank you for your love and inspiration. Thank you to my Redeem Tabernacle Church family. Thank you all for your love, prayers, support, encouragement, and blessings. You all have a special place in my heart and you all have helped me to become the woman I am spiritually and naturally.

Thank you to my Aunt Bernice. Thank you for your love, encouragement, support and prayers. Thank you for pushing me into my gift and not giving up until it came to past. Thank you for believing in me when I didn't believe in myself.

Thank you to my Uncle Steve. You have always been my supporter and believed in me in everything that I desired to do.

Thank you to my ADP family for your support and excitement for me. A special thanks to LaTonya Gibson, Trista Stephens, JaQunna Trottie, Alex Anderson, Pastor Beotis Clark, Ustace Farley, Darren Wilder, Regina Cave Moore and everyone who name I didn't list. You all have been supportive and encouraging before this journey started. May God bless you all and prosper you in your gifts.

Pastor Beotis Clark, thank you for encouraging me and allowing God to use us to be a blessing. Thank you for believing in me and praying me through the rough days. I appreciate you; you're next!

Regina Cave Moore, words cannot explain how much I appreciate you. Thank you for your hugs and smiles. Thank you for being there for me. From day one when I first told you about my book. Thank you for your vision and hard work to make this day what it is. Whatever I wanted, you made it happen. Thank you, Fairy Tales Occasions.

LaTonya Gibson, the time has finally come! Girl you know what this journey has been like. Thank you for being here for me as well as supporting my vision. I'm so grateful to have you in my life, only we know what's behind our smile. The best is yet to come and I'm so excited!

Stacie Trammell, my sister, thank you for being you. Thank you for being there for me from day one. You witnessed everything in this book plus more. When no one else knew what was going on, you were always there for me. Thanks for being my sister, friend, my ride or die. Thank you for listening, crying, laughing, shopping, everything that we have done together (even the stupid words we've shared and laughed at). I thank God for you!

Thank you LaTanya Jenkins Hunt for the photoshoot. Thank you for encouraging and praying for me. Thank you for listening to me when I felt like giving up. Thank you for listening and understanding where I was coming from. Thank you for being there for me at the last minute or whenever I needed you.

To my family and friends who are characters in this book, thank you. Thank you for allowing me to use you to share my testimony with everyone. Thank you for being a part of my life and experiences. Thank you for your support, love, and prayers. Thank you to my family and friends who are not in this book, thank you for your love and support. I love you all. Thank you to the ones who made it happened, who helped to make my dream come true, who allowed me to become a part of the Tandem Light Press amily. Thank you for working with me to get this complete. Caroline, thank you for encouraging and pushing me to dig deeper. Thank you for your patience and understanding. Pamela thank you for being patient and working with me to get my vision to come to pass. Thank you Tandem Light Press for your hard work and resources to get this book to where it needs to be. None of this would have been possible if God didn't allow us to work together. You all are awesome!

Introduction

It's Behind Her Smile is a book written from the heart and pain throughout the years. The life of a teenage girl having her first child in high school at the age of sixteen and her second child by her senior year. This book elaborates on the betrayal, pain, loneliness, emptiness, perseverance, determination and so on of a single mother. The life from teen pregnancy to single parent to an overcomer. I wrote this book to encourage others that you can make it regardless of what your situation may be. I was once at a point in my life where I thought there was no hope or better days to come.

When you put your trust in God, and give him all of you, yokes will be broken, mountains will be moved and the sun will shine again. The story of a woman who hid behind her smile for years and no one knew the pain behind it. The testimony of what God can do no matter who you are or what situation you are in. Prepare yourself to be inspired, encouraged, motivated, determined and to trust God with the faith the size of a mustard seed. What's behind your smile?

Don't Give Up

There are days in my life
When I feel like throwing
In the towel.
There are days when I feel like
I'm being punished but
don't know what for.
There are days when I feel all
odds are against me.
There are days when I just want
to lock myself in a room and just cry.
There are days when I feel as if
no-one understands or appreciates me.
When I approach these days,
I think back to where I used to be
and look at
where I am today.

I look at a wonderful husband
that God has blessed me with.
I look at my accomplishments-
marriage, family, home, education, and
variety of blessings-
I just thank God for all he has
bestowed upon me and this
makes me hold on for a little while longer.

Never give up, because the
day you give up may just be the
day God decides to send your
breakthrough.

If we look at our problems
and situations, we will actually
see how blessed we are.

Some things are not as bad as
we think they are. Sometimes,
they're better, but we're too blind
to see - we're so used to seeing the bad
side of the situation and that's what makes
it a problem or storm in our life.

The next time you feel like giving up,
look at the situation from a positive side
and give in. (You've never seen the sun
give up. Although it may rain or storm,
the sun always shines through, regardless of
what's going on in the storm. The sun always
shows up when the storm is about to start or
when it has almost destroyed the land.)

So the next time you feel like giving up,
do like the sun and shine through the storm
anyway.

Chapter 1

*I*n life, we plan for different events, success, and outcomes but God has the final plan.

Growing up as the only and oldest daughter with two younger brothers was challenging at times. My parents didn't allow me to talk on the phone with guys, hangout, or do anything that the young people were doing in my days. My childhood life consisted of going to church every Sunday, Wednesday, and sometimes throughout the week. There was no going to any school functions or participating in anything besides church.

Let me tell you a bit about my parents so you have an idea of where I come from. My dad Greg is about average height, dark and smooth chocolate colored skin tone, he's bald with a dark well-groomed beard. (I've always thought of him as handsome.) He usually worked two jobs, which called for him to be out of the house more than he wanted. Dad was and still is a hardworking man, great provider, family oriented, faithful and dedicated, strong man of God and an example of a husband, father, brother, deacon and friend. My mother Pam has smooth caramel skin, black and silky shoulder length hair and a big heart. She's willing to help and do whatever she can for others. Mom loves people and has a heart for children. She also worked — whatever her hand finds to do, she does it. Whenever mom would have to go somewhere, she would have my brothers and I stay with a family member until she was done. Even in my high school years, I had to go to a family member's house whenever my mother had to run an errand.

Honestly, my parents were strict. I felt like I couldn't do anything. Whenever I would ask to go somewhere, the answer was always "no" or "you know we don't participate in that." I use to get upset and sometimes I would cry because I felt like my life was so boring and there was nothing else to do in life but attend church. Everything was a sin. I use to say, "I can't wait to get grown, move out, and I'm definitely not going to church." I didn't know or understand what it felt like to have a normal or complete life. I didn't understand how it felt to be a teenager and enjoy my childhood.

My mother use to babysit other children so there were times when I use to have to assist her with babysitting. There were times where I used to have to watch my youngest brother all the time. With dad always working and mom was always busy doing something, there was a void in my life. I didn't know how to love or feel loved, I didn't know how to express my feelings, I didn't know how to express my love, I didn't know how to communicate. There was so much I didn't know or understand. Having a void in my life is what led me to the trials and tribulations that I faced at a young age.

August 1995 was the first day of high school. I was so excited. It was a huge moment for me—I felt like I was let loose in an open space like a child feels when she's finally allowed to go outside to play after being cooped up all winter. It was the beginning of a new chapter, and I had everything planned out. I was looking forward to meeting new people, making good grades, participating in different clubs, going to the prom and graduating. Little did I know, my life would be wildly different than what I had planned.

High school was in the country with hardly anything around but a few houses, trees and one little corner store. The school was pretty diverse even in the minimal surroundings: there were different cliques such as the hustlers, the gangsters, the hippies, duck dynasty type of people, the athletes, teen pregnancy, all kinds of students. The year started great, but quickly turned stressful when some of my schoolmates would pick on me about the way I dressed and looked. I had to wear long skirts, down to my ankles. I was not allowed to wear pants or any type of clothing that distracted the "church girl" look. If I wore a skirt that was right at or above my knee, it was considered too short. During P.E. I couldn't dress out because I wasn't allowed to wear shorts or pants so I would sneak my brothers shorts in my book bag just so I could dress out.

My classmates would ask me all the time "Why do you wear your skirts so long? Why don't you wear pants? Why do dress like an old lady?" The questions would continue daily, I would get upset and shutdown. My cousins and I would say we look like we should be characters on the show Little House on the Prairie. Some of my schoolmates were mean and harsh until they got to know me. After a few months, things started to get better and I had a few friends.

One Saturday evening in September, my cousin Stephanie and I went to the mall to hang out. Stephanie was my ride or die girl, she knew any and everything about me. I didn't have any sisters, but she felt like my big sister. Stephanie was always there for me no matter what I needed. We talked every day, all day. Stephanie was kind of shy, she was the good girl and we use to call me the bad one. She loved to sing, spend time with her dogs, and shop. Stephanie is the type of person who would brighten anyone's day. No matter what I needed, what I was going through, how I was feeling, I could (and still can) always call on her. We use to love to hang out at the mall to see how many guys we could attract or get their number.

This particular Saturday, Stephanie introduced me to this guy named Darius that went to school with her. Darius was tall, built, and had a deep voice, smooth brown skin, with an afro and tattoos. Darius was kind of shy and look liked the good innocent guy with a slightly rebellious edge. We exchanged numbers, held a conversation, and went on our way. I couldn't wait to get home so that I could call him. I was going to have to sneak and call without my parents knowing. My cousin and I came up with a plan: we would call him on three way so that our parents would think we're on the phone with each other. This was how Darius and I communicated whenever my parents were home.

Whenever I talked to Darius, he would tell me how beautiful I was, how much he loved me, and how we were going to get married after we graduated. He had me feeling like I was the most beautiful person in the world. He promised to love me forever and we would spend the rest of our life together. I fell in love with him. Well. I thought I was in love with him. He filled the void that had been chipping away at me since childhood, and that was hard to resist.

We went to different high schools and didn't see much of each other. I attended Hephzibah High and he attended Glenn Hills High School, which are about fifteen miles away from each other. After talking for a few weeks, we came up with a plan to see each other: He was to be at my house when I got home from school. My parents would be at work and I would have thehouse to myself for about forty-five minutes to an hour. I would sneak Darius in my room, we would have sex, and then we would get him out of the house before my mom came home. Everything would be back to normal by the time she got there. She wouldn't have an idea of what had taken place (at least I thought).

The plan worked the first time, second time, and actually for several months. My mom never suspected anything. It didn't take too long though, before I began to feel sick and felt as if I was gaining weight.

One day while talking and seeing Darius, I told him I was gaining weight and he told me that I was pregnant. I didn't believe him; I thought he was trying to be funny. At that time, I didn't know how a female could get pregnant. No one had ever talked to me about sex, pregnancy, boys, or anything. All I knew was that a female could get pregnant if she had sex while on her menstrual. I figured I had nothing to worry about since I wasn't having sex during my menstrual. So I was more than sure I wasn't pregnant. I remember feeling sick, I didn't know what was going on. My mom said she thought I probably had a virus, so she took me to the doctor. That's when I got the news that changed my life.

The doctor entered the room and asked me a few questions. She told me my mom could leave the room if I wanted. I agreed for my mom to leave. When she was gone, the doctor asked if I was sexually active. I told her yes and she said she was going to have to give me a pregnancy test. I wasn't prepared for this, neither was I prepared for the results. The results came back positive; the doctor said I was going to have to tell my mother because it was against the hospital policy for the doctor to tell my mother what was going on.

When my mom came into the room, the first thing she said was, "Tasha, are you pregnant?" I began to cry and told her yes. She told me not to worry, that she was going to help me get through this. I think we were both in shock. We didn't talk much on the way home. When we got there, mom asked me who got me pregnant. I told her and she said she was going to have to call his parents. I wasn't ready to go through any of this. I didn't know what the outcome would be. At the time, Darius was living with his dad. I sneaked and called him. I told him he was right, I was pregnant. I told him my mom wanted to talk to his dad to let him know what was going on. I was so nervous, I felt like my stomach was boiling butterflies on the inside. I didn't know what my life was going to be like. This was definitely not how I had planned for my freshman year of high school to be. Darius told me not to worry; he would be here for our baby and me. Darius and his dad came over to meet my parents. We had to come clean about how all of this happened. Although I was pregnant, Darius still had me feeling like he truly loved me. He promised he was going to be there for us and we would be a happy family once we graduated.

This was the beginning of a new chapter in my life and I just knew Darius and I would live "happily ever after." As I went on with my pregnancy, my classmates began to ask how it had happened. Some couldn't believe it and some would pick and say, "Church girl is having a baby."

As my pregnancy went on, my schoolmates were more respectful of me. My mother took me to all of my doctor's appointments. Darius even went to one or two of my appointments with us. I didn't meet his mother until after I had my child. My mother and cousins were supportive during my pregnancy. As I got closer to my due date, Darius started slowing down on his calling. Whenever I would call him, he was never home or he had an excuse as to why he couldn't talk at the time.

Finally, my freshman year was complete and we were out for summer break. Now I could really start preparing for my unborn child. I prepared my room with all of my baby items that people had blessed me with. I wasn't able to have a baby shower because back then it was wrong for someone to have a baby shower for a pregnant woman who conceived a baby out of wedlock. Although I didn't have a baby shower, people still blessed me with everything I was going to need for my unborn child, I had more than enough. Since I was still living with my parents, I had to share my room with my child. One side of my room was my belongings and the other side was for my baby.

On Saturday, July 26, 1997, I went into labor. Darius wasn't anywhere around. My dad drove me to the hospital and ran every red light there was. There was no need for my parents to call the ambulance because my dad held it down on his own. My mother, cousin, and grandmother met us at the hospital. Once I was admitted into the hospital and placed into the labor and delivery room, the contractions became unbearable. I was in labor all of Saturday night waiting to get this moment over. I was able to get some rest while we were all waiting. I woke up that Sunday morning in pain, I wasn't sure what was going on. The pain was worse than I'd ever imagined it could be. I felt as if someone was punching me in the abdomen with their fist. The pain was stronger and stronger as if my child was trying to come out on his own. The contractions were about four minutes apart, my dad and siblings had left late Saturday night so they could attend church on Sunday. The only people who were in the delivery room with me were my mother, my grandmother, Isabelle, and my cousin Nina. My cousin Stephanie wasn't able to come to the hospital at that time; she was home taking care of her mother. Stephanie's mother, my aunt, wasn't able to drive anymore due to her sickness. My uncle Tommy, Stephanie's dad, wouldn't bring Stephanie to the hospital. Although Stephanie wanted to be there, we both knew she wouldn't be able to and support me during labor. I don't think my uncle wanted Stephanie to partake in the results from my sin. Grandma and Nina helped coach me with pushing. They were so helpful and I was so grateful they were there.

On Sunday morning, July 27, 1997, I gave birth to a handsome and healthy baby boy, my firstborn. I was amazed that such a bundle of joy could come out of me. It was a wonderful feeling and so full of emotion. My dad and siblings came to the hospital after church to meet him. Nina had called Darius to let him know that our son was born, but he was nowhere to be found. At that time, it didn't bother me that he wasn't there to share this amazing moment with me. I was just happy to have a healthy baby boy that I was completely in love with.

After we were discharged from the hospital, three days later, my mother called Darius' mother to let her know that I had my son. To my surprise, his mother told my mother that we could take care of my son and they were going to take care of Darius' other son. Wait a minute! What? What other son? I was shocked and hurt. He never mentioned anything about another child, girlfriend, or anything. I felt like someone had stabbed me in the heart with a knife and then ran me over with an eighteen-wheeler truck. Darius' mother wanted to know what my son's blood type was and she questioned if my son was really Darius' child. She wasn't supportive at all. Whenever I would call her house looking for her son, she would tell me, "My son doesn't have time to take care of a baby. He's trying to get his education. He's going to be something in life and he don't have time for you to interfere with that." Talking about devastated. All I could think was *how in the world did I let myself get involved with someone like this let alone his mother?*

Darius would come around whenever and eventually everything stopped. No one from his side of the family was supportive or did anything to help out. My family purchased diapers, clothing, formula; whatever my son needed, they supplied. As our summer break ended, school started and it was the beginning of my sophomore year. I didn't get to start school when everyone else did. I had to wait until my six weeks were up from giving birth. When I finally did go back, my mother worked out a schedule with my cousin Linda, who is also Stephanie's sister, to babysit. Mom would drop my son off to Linda on her way to work and then pick him up after she got off. This allowed me to go to school and continue my education.

When I returned to school, my friends were excited to see me and we all had to catch up. A friend of mine, Tarika, told me about Darius' other son. Tarika was a close friend, we had a clique of four which included Tarika, Ashley, and Shola. These girls had my back no matter what. Tarika told me how my son and his half-brother were two weeks apart. Twist the knife again. I don't think I had felt that hurt to that point before in my life. The guy who promised me so much was the one who hurt me the most. Never did I imagine that he would lie and cheat on me. When I questioned him about it, he told me he never wanted to hurt me, that's why he didn't tell me. He told me how the other child's mother didn't mean anything to him and it just happened. He said the child wasn't his child and that he still wanted us to be a family. Little did I know, this was the line boys used whenever they were caught up in their lies. I decided to tell Darius that we couldn't be a couple anymore and we would never be a couple again because of the lies and hurt. He accepted and promised me that he would continue to come and see our son and take care of him. That didn't happen, it was another lie.

My sophomore year was a good and challenging year. By the end of the school year, I was adjusted to being a mom and raising my son with the support and help of my family. Darius moved on with his life and we rarely heard from him. Just when I thought the void in my life was filled, my heart was broken and I experienced my first broken heart. I had no idea of what my life would be like without him and raising my child without his father. Growing up, I hadn't known any single parents. I was used to seeing children being raised with both parents in the same home. Regardless of my circumstances, I was determined to raise my son the best way that I knew how. As I continued to go to school, I still had a void that I didn't know how or what could fill it. I remember longing for someone to love me, someone to tell me how beautiful I was, someone who would tell me that they were proud of me, someone who would make me feel worthy and appreciated.

As time continued to pass, I was still in school and getting ready to start my junior year. My cousin Linda and my aunt Elaine were still babysitting for me while I attended school. I was blessed enough to have family who supported me and was always willing to help me out the best way they could. I was glad to see that I made it further than what I expected.

In between my high school years, I continued having relationships with different guys. I was constantly looking for a guy to fill the void that I had in my life. None of those relationships lasted and meant anything. What I was searching for, they couldn't fulfill. There were times when I felt like I couldn't be by myself or alone.

As time went on, my cousins, who are twins, Tiffany and Temeka were there to help me along this journey as well. They would come over to our house, spend time with us, take us out and do whatever they could for us. My cousins would see Darius all the time, he hated to see them coming. They would ask him, "What are you up to? When was the last time you checked on your son? When was the last time you gave my cousin some money for your son? You have on new shoes; I hope you brought my little cousin some as well." They would get under his skin every time they saw him. I knew if I couldn't get him to do anything, they would definitely be the ones to get him to do right. Whenever Darius would call me, he would say "I talked to your cousins," but he would never tell me what was said. They attended the same school; I would get a report on him every day or every other day. My cousins didn't like the fact that I had to raise my son on my own, all they wanted was for Darius to do right by us. Whenever Darius saw them coming, he would try his best to dodge them but one of them would always catch him. As time went on, we just accepted how and who Darius was, we knew things would eventually catch up with him.

A Single Mother's Cry

I often sit and wonder why
He got me pregnant and said, "Goodbye"

Now I'm stuck with a baby,
And the father is somewhere with a lady

I try my best to take care of him
Now I wonder 'will the father come home?'

He does not even call to say, "How is my baby. Is he okay?"
Now I wonder who is his unlucky lady

If she knew what he put me through,
She would get up and leave him too.

I don't deserve any of this at all.

While I am at home feeding the baby, rocking
The baby, buying pampers, changing pampers,
Being frustrated, with no time for conversing, listening
To all his crying and no time for buying,

He's probably at the mall lying.

I wonder how long I will have to wait for
his call
Knowing him, he's probably somewhere having
a ball

Now I understand what my grandmother

Means when she says, "I did it all by myself,
you be strong and do it too."

"Let that boy go, he was just here to put
on a show."

You don't have time for all his lying.

Now that I understand,
I'll never do it again.

I will finish school and become somebody
I won't have to worry about any lying or crying

For all the young women who heard my
Cry,
Don't go out and listen to his lie.

Remember, it's just something they say
To get you this way.

Chapter 2

As I approached my senior year, I was glad I was of age to get my first job, which was at Food Lion. Getting a job made me feel secure and unstoppable. I felt independent because I didn't have to ask anyone to buy things for my son or ask for money. While working during the summer, I met another guy, Derrick who was my co-worker. Derrick was tall, dark skinned with a baldhead. He put me in the mind of 2Pac. He was fun to be around, had a great sense of humor, had somewhat of a thug attitude and knew when and where to turn it on and off. We would see each other and talk during our work shift. Eventually we exchanged numbers. We began to talk outside of work. Again, I would have my cousin Stephanie call him on three-way whenever my parents were home. We started sneaking around to see each other outside of work. He started buying my son any and everything as well as buying things for me. Every pay period he would go shopping for my son. I felt like there was hope: I finally met someone who's going to treat my son and I how we were supposed to be treated as a family.

He told me how beautiful I was, how much he loved my son and I, how he was going to marry me after I graduated. He promised to always be with me and take care of us like a man is supposed to take care of his family. I grew more in love with him on a daily basis. I felt complete and happy. He paid for everything that I needed for my senior year. Although my parents didn't approve of him, they appreciated that they didn't have to take care of anything financially. Once school started for my senior year, I begin to skip school so that I could be with him. Again, I didn't know or understand what birth control was and I wasn't on any. My mother had already told my nurse in the delivery room after I had my son that I wasn't going to need any birth control. My parents did not believe in birth control and my mother thought I wouldn't go down that road again of being sexually active. My mother told me that I couldn't get on any type of birth control. I never understood why she would say no regardless of what she believed or thought. The nurse said if I didn't get on any, she could promise me that she would see me back in two years having another child.

The more time I spent with Derrick, the more I thought we were going to be a family. I remember telling him one day while we were together that I needed to go to the doctor. I told him I had missed my menstrual and he was so excited. While he was excited, I was scared, nervous, and felt like my world was coming to an end. I made an appointment at the health department and to my surprise, I was pregnant. I begin to tell him this wasn't going to work, there's no way I could tell my parents that I was pregnant with my second child. This was my senior year and here I am with two children already. He promised me that I didn't have anything to worry about. He was going to take care of all of us the best way he knew how. He promised me that he wouldn't let anyone hurt or mistreat me. He promised that he would never leave me; we were going to get married. He promised he wouldn't do me the way Darius did. I believed every last promise that he made to me.

I was so afraid to tell my parents so Derrick decided he would tell them. I was worried about what people were going to think about me, how they may treat me, and how my parents were going to feel. I was afraid and depressed. I decided that I would get an abortion. I had it all planned out. I was going to get an abortion and my parents would never know. I told my grandmother Isabelle what was going on and I told her my plan. She was against it and began to encourage me not to worry about "people." She said she didn't agree with me having an abortion because she didn't believe in abortions. She said whatever I decided to do she would still be there for me. I told Derrick that I was planning on having an abortion, he told me if I did we would be over. I cried and cried because I didn't want to lose him but I couldn't imagine what my parents would do when they found out.

As I tried to carry out my plan for the abortion, Derrick and I broke up. At this time I didn't care what he thought or wanted. I figured I was doing what I needed to do for me. He dodged all of my calls and while we were at work, he wouldn't look at or say anything to me. I made my first trip for the abortion in Atlanta since I was about sixteen weeks or more. To my surprise, when I got to the abortion clinic, the receptionist asked if I had an appointment. I told her no and that I came from Augusta. She told me I was going to have to make an appointment first and I was going to have to pay in advance. I wasn't prepared for either one of those, and I was scared at the same time. I went back to Augusta and called to make my appointment. It was scheduled for that following week.

While I was waiting on time to pass by, I had all kinds of thoughts running through my mind. All I could think of is if I kept my baby, my parents were going to be upset, and people were going to talk about me. The day of my appointment for the abortion, the drive seemed long and it seemed like it was going to take forever for me to get there. When I arrived, I checked in and made my appointment. The receptionist informed me that it was going to be a two-day process. I was clueless about this whole thing. There was no way I could stay overnight in Atlanta and my parents not know where I was. She explained the process to me, the first day would be the day for the ultrasound to see how far along I truly was and then I would have to take some medicine that would put me into labor. The second day would be the day that the abortion took place. The nurse went ahead and completed my ultrasound and lab work. I remember asking her if I could see the sonogram and if she could tell me the sex of the baby, but she said it was against their policy to give me that information.

I remember thinking that I would like to at least see my child before anything took place. As I went into the waiting room to wait for the doctor to call my name to continue the process, I told the receptionist that I wasn't prepared to stay overnight. She stated that I didn't have a choice so I told her that I would reschedule and come back. On my way back to Augusta, I begin to think about my unborn child. It was during the drive back that I decided to keep my child and not worry about what "people" would say or think. Regardless of what you do in life, people will always have an opinion about you either negative or positive.

When I made it back to Augusta, I told my grandmother that I decided to keep my child; I didn't want an abortion. She was excited, not for the fact that I was pregnant but for the fact that I didn't have the abortion. She said if anything would have happened to me while I was on the abortion table, there's no way she would be able to have peace knowing she knew I was going to do it. She told me not to worry about my parents being upset, she would let them know. Later on that day, I called Derrick and told him that I decided not to have the abortion. He was so excited, and immediately asked if we could get back together and be a family. Of course my answer was yes! I knew I wouldn't have anything to worry about. He was going to be a great dad. I'd watched how he took good care of my son and he wasn't even his biological child. My thought was: if he's taking such good care of my child that's not his biological, I could only imagine how he would take care of our unborn child.

I eventually told my mom and again like the first time, she told me not to worry she's going to help me out. She told me my dad was going to be upset and that I needed to tell him. I told mom who the daddy was and she asked how did this happen. Really it all happened from me sneaking behind my parents back. All of my darkness was revealed in the light. Derrick again volunteered to tell my dad, and I agreed to let him. He came over to our house one day and met with my dad. He told my dad that he was going to take care of his child as well as my son and I. My dad still didn't agree with Derrick coming around or anything.

Derrick took me to majority of my doctor's appointments. He was there for me for my whole pregnancy. On Sunday morning, July 18, 1999, I woke up in pain. This time I knew what was taking place; I knew I was in labor. I went into my parent's room and told them what was going on. My mother called the doctor to let him know that I was having contractions and to see if I needed to come in. My dad and siblings had left to go to church and mom was there in charge. My mom also called my cousin Stephanie and Linda to let them know that I was in labor. Linda and Demetria, a friend of the family, came over to assist us. At that time, my cousin Nina, my younger cousins who were also twins were at our house. Mom had to call my cousin Leah who is the twin's mom to come pick them up since I was in labor. Nina called Derrick to let him know that I was in labor and he came over to our house as well. My mother drove us to the hospital all I could say to myself was, "Man, I wish my dad was here to take me to the hospital. I would've been at the hospital by now." Mom stopped at every red light and she stopped by my aunt's church to let her know that we were headed to the hospital. This was the longest ride ever.

It's Behind Her Smile

This was a day I had been waiting for, I was afraid that my child would be born with health issues as God's way of punishing me for having the thought of wanting to have an abortion. My state of mind at that time was that God was going to punish me for all of my sins and I had cursed my unborn child. Not only was I sinning but I was lost and didn't have a relationship with God or even really knew him. I went into labor and gave birth to a beautiful and healthy baby girl. I was happy and overwhelmed with joy to see my baby.

I had a chance to experience what it was like to have my child's dad in the labor and delivery room with me. He even spent the night with me in the hospital. He assisted with whatever I needed while I was in the hospital. Once we were discharged from the hospital, Derrick would come over to make sure we were okay. There were times where he would even pick my daughter up so she could spend the night and I could rest. It felt like my little world was becoming my dream come true. Derrick was doing any and everything he could to make sure we were taken care of.

As time went on and my daughter began to get older, Derrick began to change. He could barely hold down a job and he became jealous. He was always jealous of people who blessed my children with things especially things that he couldn't afford. He would get upset and tell me to tell everyone to stop buying for my children—that was his job. He started cheating on me. I found out later he had been doing that all along. He started lying to me all the time and he quickly became a person whom I had never met. He would accuse me of cheating on him just to justify what he was doing to me. He would tell me that no one would want to be with me, especially since I had two children by two different men. He would tell me he was going to take my daughter from me and move to Florida. He would tell me that he wasn't going to have any other man taking care of his child. He would constantly threaten me and would try to make me feel as low as he was.

After I told him I no longer wanted to be with him, he called me every name in the book. He told me if he left, my daughter was going with him. He tried everything that he could think of to make me feel guilty for not wanting to stay in a relationship with him. He tried to destroy my self-esteem and make me feel as if no one else would ever date or marry me. Once Derrick realized that we were no longer going to be a couple, he proposed to me to see if that would change my mind. He knew that marriage was something that I always wanted and dreamed of. He knew that I took marriage serious and that whoever I married, I would be a great wife to him. At that time, I no longer cared about being married, being with him, or having the life that I desired to have with him. I was tired of being verbally abused; that hurt more than anything. I felt and knew that I deserved better than what I had and what I was dealing with. My life and children were more important than an engagement ring and a dead relationship. I knew it was time for me to move forward in my life and not stay in a relationship that wasn't worth having. I began to believe at eighteen that I would never find anyone and no man would ever find and chose me to be his wife (how sad is that?!). I thought every relationship that I got in, would always end in me getting hurt.

Two months after we broke up, Derrick decided to move out of the state. I never got a chance to meet any of his family. I talked with his mother and sister over the phone a couple of times. His family never got a chance to meet my daughter; they lived in California and Texas. They knew about her, but never met or did anything for her. Before Derrick moved to Florida, he went and got a tattoo on his neck with my daughter initials and birthdate on one side of his neck and got her name on the other side of his neck. I couldn't understand how he could just up and move away like that because I no longer wanted to be with him. Everything that he had told and promised me was a lie. People can live a lie for a little while, but the truth of the person will always be revealed. I always wondered how he could wake up every morning, see our daughter's name on his neck and not reach out or do anything for her.

After Derrick moved to Florida, I heard from him for a few months. Whenever he called, he would still try his best to make me feel bad for making the decision to cut our relationship off. His calls were never about our daughter; they were always about me and whether or not I had found someone. Derrick tried his best to make sure nothing good would happen for me. He figured as long as he wasn't taking care of my children and giving me money for things that I needed, I wouldn't have a choice but to stay with him. He promised he would send gifts and boxes of things for my children every month since he no longer lived close by. I never received those items, and before long, I didn't hear from him at all.

I was happy I was able to graduate. I graduated right before I had my daughter and that made me happy. I was ready to move on with my life. I began looking for employment so that I could take care of my children and show Derrick that I could make it without him.

The Man I Love

The man I love
betrayed me.
The man I love
misled me.
The man I love
hurt us.
The man I love
turned against us.
The man I love
turned his back on us.
The man I love
let us down
The man I love
cheated on me.
The man I love
didn't want me.
The man I love
chose someone else over me.
The man I love,
where did he go?
how did he do it?
when did he fade away?
The man I love,
hey, I guess I'll never know.

Chapter 3

*W*ork didn't come easily, and as time passed, I began to wonder how I was going to provide for my children and I. Since Derrick and I were no longer together, I had to take care of us from now on. I have some family who lived in a small town called Waynesboro, Georgia, they told me they could help me find a job there. I decided to take them up on their offer and move to Waynesboro. While there, my cousins introduced me to this guy named Edward. Edward was tall, built, brown skinned, low cut haircut, a little shy around a group of people, had a sense of humor, and was a hustler in the streets. We all began to hang out. Edward and I decided to start spending more time alone together. We talked about what each of us had been through in past relationships. I wasn't really ready for a new relationship since I had recently gotten out of one. It hadn't even been six months since my last relationship. As I shared with him what I had gone through, he asked if I could give him a chance. Once again, I said yes.

We began to discuss our plans for our relationship; we both wanted the relationship to work. I found an apartment for us. Once again, he promised to take care of and provide for my children and I. He promised not to take me through anything like what I'd been through with my past two relationships. I believed everything that he told me; I didn't think I would have a problem with this relationship. Again I was trying to fill this void that I had and I felt like I needed a man to complete me as well as take care of us. I didn't believe that I could take care of two children by myself. I thought that was impossible.

After moving in together, we started working together on the same shift. We both left that employer and started working for a different manufacturing company. We worked both shifts: he worked first shift and I worked second shift. My mom would keep my children for me during the week and we would have them on the weekends since we were off. It seemed as if we had a perfect relationship in the beginning; one that I had desired for the longest time. He provided for us and helped me out with my children. Things were going great and I knew we were on the right track.

I got pregnant with my third child, which made Edward baby daddy number three. I replayed my past two pregnancies in my head over and over, hoping that this pregnancy and relationship wouldn't end like the past two. I suppose I was a little traumatized after both Derrick and Darius had disappeared after I had their babies.

It was time for my mother to return to work from the summer break so my children moved in with me permanently. Mom had them for about two to three months. Mom asked Edward if he would be able to take care of us and if he was sure that he would treat us right. He promised her that he could and would and that she didn't have anything to worry about. He promised to be the best man and father that he could be and said my parents could trust him with us.

I ended up quitting my job so that I could stay home and raise my children and focus on our unborn child. A month or two had passed and I started noticing a change in Edward's routine. While it seemed as if he was family orientated, that began to change. He would stay out some nights, sometimes past one or two in the morning. Sometimes after work he wouldn't come straight home and if it was the weekend, he would get off work and stay gone until Sunday. He would always have some excuse (or should I say lie). I would go along, but deep down inside, I knew he was lying and something wasn't right. I tolerated the

foolishness because I was pregnant with my third child and by this time, I truly believed that no one would want me
.

As time went on, I took myself to my prenatal appointments. Edward went a few times but the majority of the time I went by myself. One of my cousins, Leah, was also pregnant with her third child at the same time that I was. We would ride together to some of our appointments, then go shop for the babies. I felt like I had someone there with me and someone who understood me. I felt like Edward wasn't a part of this pregnancy with me so I looked forward to seeing Leah and sharing our experiences. She was a comfort to me.

Leah went into labor about a week or two before I did and I was excited for her and alone at the same time. I didn't have a baby shower; everything that I had for my unborn child came from family and the money that I was saving. Neither Edward nor his family helped purchase anything. Edward was barely home or spent time with us. I began to see that this relationship wasn't going to work either; it was just a matter of time before I ended it.

One Wednesday morning on May 23, 2001, the pain from contractions woke me up. I was in labor so I woke Edward up so that we could go ahead and drive to Augusta, which was thirty to forty-five minutes away from Waynesboro. I called my mother to let her know that we were on our way to Augusta and to meet us at the hospital. As always, my mother was there to help. She met us half way to get my two other children so that Edward could get me to the hospital and focus on me. Mom and my children came to the hospital once I was admitted.

I went into labor and gave birth to a healthy and handsome baby boy. It was an exciting day for me. My family was there for support as usual, but once again, no one from Edward's family was there. Edward was there for me during my stay in the hospital. Although this was a special day for me, I knew deep down inside that our relationship was going to be over soon. That day I realized I deserved better and I was going to do whatever I had to do to take care of my children. I wasn't going to rely on a man any longer to fill my void or to make me happy, and I certainly wasn't going to rely on man to take care of my children.

After being discharged from the hospital, things began to go back to normal. Normal for us consisted of me being home, raising my children, cooking, cleaning, and waiting for Edward to call or come home. The same day that I was discharged from the hospital, Edward left to go hang out with his homeboys. He told me he had some errands to run and he would be back to help me get settled in. Edward hung out with his friends and stayed out instead of being home with us.

Whenever Edward was home, he would write songs and say he was going to the studio; he's going to become a rapper. I would read some of his songs and he would talk about one of his other baby mamas and I. He would write about how he's living with me and messing around with her. There were all kinds of signs that I ignored. There were times when I would find other females phone numbers, females would call his phone, and I would hear different things about other females from people who knew we were together. Edward even allowed another woman to come into our home while I was at my uncle's funeral one day.

During the holidays, he would never spend the day with us. He would always say he had somewhere to go and would tell me he'd be right back. He would never buy anything for me or my children for holidays or occasions. My mom would get information for me to help get Christmas items for my children during the holidays. I was appreciative of whatever the "Christmas helpers" would bless us with. I would go to Family Dollar and Wal-Mart to buy whatever I could to add to the other items I had already received. What brought joy to my heart on Christmas was seeing the happiness on my children's faces when they opened their gifts. It didn't matter how much it cost or where it came from, they were just happy, and I truly couldn't ask for anything better.

Things began to go downhill in our relationship; I suffered with anxiety attacks due to stressing. I suffered from anxiety attacks so much, I could always feel when I was about to have one. I would began to have shortness of breath, tingling in my fingers, heart fluttering, and I would have hot flashes all of sudden. I was in an unhealthy and stressful relationship. I started having feelings of leaving Edward but I started to believe that no one would want me with three children by three different men. Edward would constantly tell me that I wouldn't be anything without him, no one is going to look at or even want me, I would never find anyone and the list goes on.

While debating on what I was going to do with myself and waiting to see how our relationship was going to go, I enrolled myself into Waynesboro Technical College. I wasn't sure what I was doing or how I was going to do it but I knew I wanted to attend college. My grandmother lived in Waynesboro, she told me she would babysit my children while I attend school. My first-born was enrolled in HeadStart for three year olds and my other two children stayed with my grandmother while I attended classes. I didn't have any support from Edward, it was like he was trying to hold me back to keep me from becoming successful. I would have to take my son to school, drop my other children off to my grandmother's and then I would head to class. After my classes, I would have to pick my children up and then go home and try to prepare dinner and help my son with homework. Once dinner was done and everyone had eaten, my son's homework was complete, my children had a bath and were in the bed, that's when I would have some down time to try to complete my homework. There were nights when Edward wouldn't come home and when he did get home, he was high or drunk, sometimes both. He wasn't any help or supportive to me at all. Anxiety attacks began to attack my body, Edward would tell my parents that it was school and my children who were stressing me out. He would never tell them it was him, I'm sure they knew the truth. I felt as if I was going to have a break down at any moment.

The stress level continued to rise and I finally was getting tired of being verbally and mentally abused, I wanted to get out of that relationship. Edward started having women to come pick him up from our apartment to take him to work. There were plenty of mornings when he thought I was sleep when he got ready to leave for work and as soon as he walked out of the door, I would jump out of the bed and peek out of the window just to see how he was getting to work. I had a car and license but he didn't have either. I would see the same car and woman come pick him up several mornings and when I would ask him how he got to work, he would say "my homeboy."

I started making plans to leave him. I saved every penny that I received, I searched for an apartment so that I could move back to Augusta, and I told my family I was going to move out and leave him. When I told Edward that I was getting tired and wanted to leave, he proposed to me. He knew that I wanted to get married and be a family, proposing was his way of keeping me. I had mention marriage to him in the earlier part of our relationship and he would tell me we couldn't get married because we couldn't afford it and he didn't have the money he needed. It was funny to me that he didn't want to get married before but now that I was talking about leaving, that's when he wanted to propose. He asked for another chance to work things out and prove to me he was serious. I told him I would give him another chance and then we'll see where the relationship would go. Well, things didn't get any better between us and the anxiety attacks kept attacking me.

I was so messed up because I believed the lies about no one wanting me, I wouldn't be able to raise three children by myself, I would never be anything. I was told a woman with three children by three different guys would never make it in this world. I struggled in my mind with those lies, they were my biggest hindrance. I knew that I deserve more and better than this, I just needed to figure out how to have enough courage to leave regardless of my situation. I was afraid to move because I didn't have a job and I knew my savings was going to run out eventually out. At this moment, I didn't care, I would figure everything else out later. I just wanted to be out of this relationship and get on with my life. I found an apartment in Augusta, submitted my application, and paid my deposit. After receiving my move in date, I began to prepare for freedom.

One Friday while Edward was at work, I had everything all planned out. That morning when he left for work, I jumped out of bed and began packing. I had people lined up to help me make this transition and to make it within eight hours. I had a cousin named Chris who drove the U-haul truck for me and I had a couple who lived a few doors down from us to come help me pack and load the truck. Edward was unaware of everything that had taken place and the things to come. I felt as if he had treated me so bad, lied and cheated, why should I tell him I was leaving.

Within four to five hours, we had the apartment empty and the truck was loaded. I was shocked myself to see how fast we moved and gotten everything taken care of. Once we got everything from Waynesboro to Augusta, I had family in Augusta waiting for our arrival so they could help get me situated into my new apartment. The only thing I left in the apartment in Waynesboro was Edward belongings. I felt like a burden was lifted and I was finally free, I didn't have to worry about anyone mistreating me or my children. This was the day of my breakthrough, the day of getting myself together.

As I began to unload and unpack, time began to fly bye. I hadn't heard anything from Edward, it was after 5pm so he should've been off by then. I knew Edward must have not went by the apartment yet because he would've seen how empty the apartment was with nothing but his belongings waiting by the door. I didn't hear anything from him that Friday, it was on a Monday morning when I finally heard from him. That weekend confirmed why I was happy I was out of that apartment and relationship with him. For him to call me that Monday morning, that meant he didn't go home at all that weekend just like he had done several times before.

When he called, he cursed me out, threaten me, and tried his best to tear me down. I didn't let any of that bother me. He began to tell me how I'll never be anything, I'll never have anything, I'll never get married, I'll never make it without him and the list goes on. I could care less about the words that he was speaking to me, it didn't matter anymore. I was confident in myself and was determined not to let Edward verbally abuse me anymore. As time went on, Edward realized I didn't need him, he needed me. The more he saw I was becoming independent again, he would beg me to give us another chance and promised he would treat me better than what he had been treating me. I didn't give in or take him back, I was glad to be free and single. It was time for me to focus on my three children, find a job and make sure we were taken care of.

When it Hurts....

When it hurts most,
you feel as if the whole world is against you
When it hurts most,
you feel as if your dreams can't come true
When it hurts most,
you feel as if you're in this dark room alone
When it hurts most,
you feel as if you have no one
When it hurts most,
you feel as if everyone is gone but you, and you are left alone

When it hurts most,
you feel as if your heart is beating
but nothing is coming out

Chapter 4

LaTasha S. Woodcock

After getting settled into my apartment and getting a grip on things, I started applying for jobs. I told my cousin Tiffany who worked for RaceTrac that I was looking for a job. Tiffany was able to get me hired on with RaceTrac as well, it was an exciting feeling to finally be working again, I felt as if I had won the lottery. Getting hired at RaceTrac was going to help me get my independence back and take care of my babies. My mother would babysit for me while I work. I was working and taking classes as well. Although I had moved to Augusta, I was still driving back and forth to Waynesboro to attend Waynesboro Technical College. I began to get worn out by driving back and forth to Waynesboro, working, taking care of my children, helping with homework and the list goes on. There were times when I would dose off at the wheel from being tired and not getting any rest because of my schedule. I was determined not to let this stop me from reaching my goals. I transferred my classes to Augusta Technical College Campus, which would be more convenient for me.

While attending ATC, there were times when I would have to work double shifts at RaceTrac, sometimes I had to work the third shift and once I got off that next morning I would have to be in class by eight thirty. There were times when I had to work doubles and the manager would tell me if I couldn't work a double shift, they may not keep me hired on there. I needed that job, that was income to take care of my children and bills. There were times when I had to clean the public restroom on my shift. Although it was a public restroom, I would clean it as if it was my own. I learned to do what I had to do to take care of my own. Cleaning the restroom, stocking the cooler, cleaning and mopping inside of the store, taking out the trash as well as taking out the trash from the trashcans in the parking lot and sweeping the trash off the ground was my duties as well. There were times when it would get overwhelming but I had three mouths to feed; I didn't focus so much on myself.

I applied for the second shift manager position but I didn't get it, one thing I learned was that when you are denied something, there's always something greater coming. About two weeks after the announcement of me not getting the position, the District Manager met with me to offer me a Floating Manager position. He told me what was required and the benefits, this was better than the position I was denied, plus a greater increase in my paycheck. I rotated shifts between Augusta, Aiken, South Carolina, and Thompson, Georgia. There was exhaustion and plenty of long nights. There were times when I had to work the third shift. My dad was working part time delivering newspapers and he would stop by to check on me sometimes. There were nights when he stopped by and I had fallen asleep on the job. The doors would be locked at night so dad would knock on the window to get my attention. He would always tell me that I needed to find somewhere else to work, he didn't like me working the night shift by myself.

While working and attending classes, I began to want to experience something other than the normal so I started hanging out at the club. There were times when I would go to the club Wednesday thru Sunday, if I didn't make it on Wednesday, I started on Thursday. My cousins Tiffany and Temeka, would go to the club with me. Temeka and I use to call Tiffany grandma at times because she would be sleepy and fall asleep early so she wouldn't be able to hang out with us. The times that Tiffany didn't want to go to the club with us, she would babysit my children for me so that I could go out. Whenever Tiffany couldn't babysit, I would have my youngest brother Charlie to come over to spend the night so that he could babysit. I started meeting different guys and dating for fun. I wasn't looking for anyone in particular or a relationship period, I just wanted someone to chill with. I had my share of meeting different guys as well as having someone who would be my cutbuddy for a short time. Darius had gone into the Navy and he was home to visit. I hadn't seen or heard from him for about a year or two. When he first went into the Navy, his mother told me he was moving on with his life and she wasn't going to let me stop him or my oldest son keep him from going into the Navy. She tried her best to keep him away from us. I ran into Darius at the club, he told me what he had been up to and was questioning my life at that time and my relationship status. He told me he was home visiting for a while and he would be leaving back out soon. We exchanged numbers and I gave him my address.

Whenever I moved or changed numbers, I tried my best to contact my children's father to give them information just so they could have a way of contacting me and they couldn't have any excuses for not taking care of their child. Darius told me he would write me once he returned to his station if it was okay with me. One particular letter he sent me, he apologized for everything he had done to me in the past, he even apologized for the way his mother treated me. At the end of the letter, he said he don't think he would ever find a woman like me; I was doing a great job raising my children and asked if I would marry him. I wrote him back to tell him how I felt and the pain he took me through. I also told him I couldn't accept his proposal. He wrote me back to see if I would change my mind, he said he needed me. Changing my mind was one thing that I couldn't do again. I had moved on with my life and I couldn't go backwards.

While I was still clubbing and enjoy myself, I was still working, attending classes, taking care of my children and whatever else we had going on. Edward was still calling and asking for another chance but I could never give in. He would get my two youngest children on the weekend or whenever he had time. He would lie and tell me he's not dating anyone, he's trying to get himself together so he could win his family back. Edward would constantly ask me if I was involved with anyone and I would tell him no.

One particular day during the summer, I had some guys over as well as my homegirls, Edward popped up at my apartment. I didn't want him to come in because I didn't want any drama and I didn't want him to make a scene like he would normally do. Things got heated and he came into my apartment and took my youngest son. He jumped on me and took off with our son. My homegirl called the police and my family, Edward called my dad and told him don't believe anything that I tell him. He said he didn't kidnap my son, he was getting him for a while, he told my dad that he didn't jump on me. He lied to my dad about everything. There were marks on my neck and stomach from where Edward had pushed me and made me fall as well as chocked me and pushed me over a wooden rail that was in front of my apartment. When the officers arrived at my apartment, Edward was already gone with my son. The officers wrote up the report, took pictures and talked to me and everyone who was there that witness the incident. One of the officers asked for Edward number so that he could contact him and tell him to return my son. I called Edward mother and told her what was going on and to have Edward to call me and return my son. Edward called and met with my dad so he could return my son because he had found out the officers were trying to contact and locate him. He dodged the police because he didn't want to be arrested. After the report was taken, I was told to go to 401 which was our local police station and file a report. After filing the report, I was given a court date but I didn't attend court when the time had come. I was glad that moment was behind me and I didn't want to relive that moment again. It was hurtful because the guy who once claimed he loved and would never hurt me, end up abusing me not only verbally but physically. Time had passed since all of this had taken place, I was still enjoying my single life. Edward started coming around, paying child support, getting our son for the weekend sometimes longer, and helping out whenever he could. He was trying his best to get another chance and prove to me he wanted us to work. I was completely done with Edward, there was no way we could ever work out again.

In between working, attending classes and raising my children, I was clubbing every chance I got. I met different guys, I even got into a relationship or two. I didn't stay in those relationships long because I couldn't get over my past relationships and I couldn't trust guys anymore. I use to think all guys are alike and none of them couldn't be trusted. My life became so hectic. I slowed down on hanging out and started chilling out at home. When everything was stable again, I started the club life once again until it became old to me. I was tired of hearing the same pickup lines, seeing the same people, doing the same thing and getting the same results. I wanted more in life than to club, work, school and dating different guys.

I wanted to show my family and friends that I could do just what they said I couldn't do and I could have what they said I couldn't have. I continued working, there were times when I had to work double shifts. I continued to pursue my education at Augusta Technical College until I had to stop for a season. I continued doing what I had to do to take care of my three children, although I was tired at times, I didn't let that stop me.

I figured if I didn't work, I couldn't provide for my children, neither would anyone else provided for them the way that I did. I also didn't want to depend on anyone or ask anyone for anything. I applied for food stamps, housing, and welfare but was denied benefits from everything I applied for. I was told that I made too much money, which I was confused. I would see how females were getting assistance and taking advantage of the system but here I was busting my butt to take care of mine and I couldn't get assistance. I felt like as I long as I was trying to help myself and rise above my situation, I couldn't get any help but the females who wasn't trying to do anything with themselves were the ones who received all the benefits. I kept applying for assistance as I was finally able to get food stamps after showing my lowest paystub. The food stamps helped me out a lot and came in handy.

LaTasha S. Woodcock

The Virus

There's this virus going around
We don't know who started it.
There was this woman clean and clear
From it all
Until one night this man caught
It and brought it home.
She did all she could to keep from
Catching it
Some kind of way she was
Hit.
She loved him,
Cared for him,
Was his backbone,
Tried to be strong,
Respected him,
Never misled him,
Comforted him,
Never confronted him,
Gave him her all,
Didn't get a chance to make it
To the mall.
Let him in her wing
Never once did she see that ring.
She's still researching, trying to figure out
Where and who started this virus
Now her research is done, this is what she
Discovered
"The man she loved didn't love her
Enough so that she could become his queen."
He cheated with this beast

It's Behind Her Smile

Who just wanted some green.
He never appreciated or loved her,
So the beast stepped in and hated
The beast tried so hard to catch him,
He ended up letting her fetch him.
He went out on a night of town
Not one time did the queen fool around
He drank some poison that
Caused him a future
He caught the virus from the beast
Who caught the virus from the least
The virus is called "Cheating"
Now where's the beast that started
the beating?
The virus caused pain, suffering, loneliness,
Stress, hurt, broken hearts, weakness,
A bucket of tears, fears, desertion, misleading,
Confusion and abuse

The virus caused so many distractions,
It would take all day to come up
With a fraction.
Queens be careful and watch out for
This virus.
You never know where the
Symptoms are.

On the alert for the beast
And frog with the virus called "Cheating"
A (none) vaccine and incurable disease
Once you catch it, you will always have it.

Chapter 5

LaTasha S. Woodcock

*I*t was 2004, I was content with working and raising my children and just living my life. My cousins and friends had moved on with their life and everyone was doing their own thing. One night I decided to go to the club for a few hours, it had been about a year and some months since I went to the club. I decided to go to the club with a friend of mine at the time, I really didn't feel like being bothered, I was there just to enjoy myself. As the music was playing and everyone in the club seemed to be having a great time, I had a headache and was ready to go. I met this guy name Harold who was interested in me but I didn't feel like being bothered or listening to whatever lies he was going to tell me. Harold was dark skinned, built, smooth skin, clean cut haircut, respectful, and welled dressed. I called him my Idris Elba, he was the complexion and had the accent of Idris. He also had a thuggish style to him as well but not to the point of I had to watch my back around him. I eventually broke down and started talking and listening to him. I had a terrible headache and I was ready to leave, he offered to take me to the store to purchase something for my headache but I turned down the offer. I didn't know him like that to trust him enough to take me anywhere.

That night at the club, Harold and I went and sat in his car so we could talk. He told me as we were walking outside that he didn't drive a nice car or a car with rims or anything. It didn't matter to me what kind of car Harold drove, I was happy he had a license and a car. We talked for a few hours until our friends were ready to leave. We talked about relationships, things that we were dealing with and so on. We both felt comfortable by the end of the night, we felt as if a friendship was established that night. He told me that he was hesitant about talking to me because I seemed like the type of female who had it all together and only dated suit and tie guys. He said I was pretty to him, most guys would call me sexy. He didn't think I would give him any time or even talk to him. I wasn't looking or wanting to be in a relationship, I was enjoying being a single parent. We started being "cut buddies", which is the term we used back in the day which means sex partners no matter what. We were cut buddies for a few months until he decided to leave me alone.

We would see each other in passing every now and then. I was still enjoying my life and children. I wasn't involved in a relationship. There were several times when I would go to work and one of my co-workers would tell me that a guy had been coming to my job looking for me. I never knew who it was or why this guy would be looking for me. I began to ignore the thought and didn't care who it was. One particular day, January 12, 2005, while driving to work, I thought about my cut buddy, Harold. I was wondering what he was up to, where he was, and whether or not he was still living in Augusta. I had said to myself that I would call his last known place of employment to see if he still worked there. When I got to work, I was busy and didn't think about calling Harold. I got so caught up in work, I never did get a chance to call. While at work, I received a phone call that same day from Harold, who I was thinking about on my way to work. I shared with him how it was funny to me that I was planning to call him but he beat me to We talked for a few minutes and exchanged current numbers and we began to talk more after I got off work that night. We talked and talked and talked, trying to catch up on what we had been up to since we last talked to each other. It was January 15, Harold's birthday. I decided to surprise him after I got off of work. I went to his job and surprised him with a birthday cake and card; he was so happy and surprised. That was Harold's first birthday cake. He wasn't expecting to receive anything for his birthday. I stayed at his job with him for a few minutes until it was time for me to go pick up my children. We talked later on that day after he got off from work. We continued to talk and spend time together. We discussed what we wanted in the future. We were at a mature stage in our life and with each other. We decided to take our friendship further and become a couple. Harold and my children had never met, that's one thing that I said I would stop doing whenever I met a guy. I didn't want my children to keep seeing guys in and out of our life and Harold also agreed not to meet my children until we decided that our relationship would be official and taken more seriously; we made plans for my children to meet Harold. I took them to his house where we ate, talked, and watched movies. Harold left the room to do something and my oldest son Marquis looked at me and said, "Mom, I like him; he can be our stepdaddy." I knew then that he had to be the one, my grandmother use to tell me that a child can feel if a person is a good person or not and if I ever dated someone and my children would like him, he's the one.

On February 24, 2005, which was my birthday, we decided to move in together. I was nervous and scared at the same time because of my experience I had in the past of living with Edward. I decided to just go along with it and see how it would work and rather or not we would last. As we moved into our first place together, things were going perfect for us. I was happy and confident about what we had going on. There were certain situations that arose, but we were still determined to make our relationship work.

I was working at Raceway by this time because RaceTrac was sold to Raceway. I was one of the few associates that transition. Harold was working two jobs as usual—he is always hard-working. My oldest son and daughter were in school and my grandmother was babysitting my youngest son. My dad was working in Waynesboro and would pick Eric up for me every morning and drop him off to my grandmother's house on his way to work. My children and I didn't see Harold as much due to our schedules. While my children were at school, Harold would be home sleeping since he would be getting off in the mornings. When my children and I were home, Harold would be working; he worked twelve-hour shifts. In between his jobs, he would do whatever he could to help me out around the house and with my children.

One Sunday, my children and I went to church with a close friend of mine named Toy. The service was good and everyone was worshipping and praising God. During the service, I began to have hot flashes, feeling light headed, weak and nauseated. As the pastor got ready to get up and preach, I remember sitting down and vomiting. I began sweating and feeling weak. I couldn't move. Toy called Harold to have him to come pick me up from church. I assumed I had a virus and had ate something that got me sick. I had to go to work later on that day, when I arrived at work I told my manager what was going on. While I was talking to him, I got weak again and felt like I had to vomit. My manager asked me if I was pregnant, I looked at him and laughed. That moment was funny to me because that was the last thing that I was thinking that could be wrong. In 2002, the doctor had told me there was a chance of not being able to have any more children. I never questioned why because it didn't matter to me at the time; I didn't want anymore.

Harold and I had discussed having a child together, but he knew that I couldn't have anymore. I told him several times that if I could have more children, we could try to get pregnant if we decided to get married. Harold told me it would be nice to have at least one child with me, but he understood that I couldn't have anymore. We had even talked about considering adopting a baby since I couldn't have any more children. Later on that night, after I got off from work, Harold and my brother Charlie kept saying that I was pregnant and I laughed at them. I told them that I had a virus and there was no way in the world I could be pregnant. They laughed at me and decided to make a bet, the bet was one hundred dollars apiece if I found out that I was pregnant. Me being sure that I wasn't, I told them to go to the store to buy a pregnancy test. When they got back from the store, they had three pregnancy test for me. Before I took the test, I told them that they were crazy to think that I was pregnant.

I took the test and to my surprise, the test read POSITIVE. I sat in the bathroom for a few minutes and cried. I was in complete disbelief. For three years I'd had my share of sex partners and not one time did I get pregnant because I couldn't (well that's what I thought). I was pregnant with my fourth child, I was emotionally drained and felt like giving up. I felt like everything people had said about me in a negative manner was going to come true. It felt like I kept giving my all to these guys and the only thing that I was getting in return was a baby. I had no hope or trust in Harold, in the back of my mind, I was sure he was going to do the same thing the other three baby daddies had done to me. I pulled myself together and left the bathroom to go share the news with my boyfriend and brother.

As I shared the news, my brother laughed and asked for his one hundred dollars — to this day, I still owe him. Harold hugged me and told me everything was going to be all right. I didn't believe him. There was a big difference about my boyfriend at that time: he didn't promise me those same lies like the others had. He decided to let his actions speak for itself. Although we were going through some rocky moments, he proposed to me in August of that year. He got off work one day, and while I was in the kitchen cooking and helping my children complete their homework, Harold snuck up behind me. I didn't know what was going on or why my children were excited, I thought they were just happy to see him. Harold grabbed my hand, pulled out a ring, and asked me to marry him. I said yes and he just held me. In the back of my mind, I was still doubting his love for me and whether or not we would last. People couldn't believe that we were going to get married and many voiced their own fears of us being together long-term.

My mother was so happy that I was finally getting married and she helped me planned for our big day. Although it wasn't the wedding that I dreamt of having, we were still getting married. I always wanted to have a fairytale wedding—a girl's dream. I wanted a wedding in a mega church with hundreds of people. I'd a wedding planned out since the age of ten. That dream didn't matter to me anymore. Everyone told me I would never get married but that was a lie. I was seven months pregnant when we got married and my stomach was huge; I was just happy to be getting married.. My grandmother was also very happy for me and helped purchase my wedding gown. We planned our wedding for October 22, 2005.

I had mixed emotions on our wedding day, mostly because I was still doubting what we had. I felt like I was dreaming all of this was happening. We didn't have the perfect wedding or the perfect reception but we had each other. We didn't go on a honeymoon then, but we said we would plan for one later on in life. The night of our wedding, we both were tired and ready to get some rest. I was huge like a cow and swollen. I just wanted to get home, shower, and go to bed.

LaTasha S. Woodcock

After the wedding was over, we had to get ready for our unborn child. Our life was passing by fast, we started dating in January, we moved in our place together in February, I got pregnant, Harold proposed in August and we got married in October — all in the same year. Talk about a whirlwind romance.

On December 3, 2005, I was awakened by the urge to use the restroom. My husband was at work and my children were asleep. By the time I came out of the restroom, Harold called to check on me. He asked how I'd slept that night and if I was in labor. At the time, I didn't know I was in labor, so I told him no. A few minutes after we got off the phone, I began to have contractions. I woke my children to get them dressed. I showered and got everyone ready to go to my parents' house. As I drove to my parents' house, the contractions came stronger. When we arrived, I told my mother that I thought I might be in labor. She went to the room to get my dad, then called my husband and the doctor. My doctor stated that I needed to come in, I was in labor. Harold told my mother that he would meet us at the hospital. My dad drove me to the hospital for the second time. He'd driven me with my oldest son and now my youngest son, and we share a bond because of that.

As the nurse, my dad and I were getting off of the elevator, my husband was walking in excited to see me. I was in pain, but I was happy to see my husband there with me. He made sure that I was comfortable and okay. By the time the nurses got me prepared to give birth, I had dilated to eight centimeters and I was too far out to receive an epidural. The pain was so severe that I felt like someone was punching me in my abdomen with a light pole. After several pushes, our son was born. I was tired but happy at the same time. My husband kissed me and told me that I had done a great job and thanks for a healthy baby.

My husband and I had already discussed getting my tubes tied; we didn't want any more children. The doctors tied my tubes right after I had given birth. By the time they were finished, I was drained and just wanted to rest. My husband was there with me through everything and attended to our son while I rested. After two days in the hospital, I was discharged and ready to go home.

There were moments of nervousness and anxiety after we got home; I felt it was just a matter of time before my husband left me to raise all four of my children alone. My panic caused us both to snap at one another, but we were still determined to make our marriage work. We were determined to work our issues out regardless of how big or small.

A few days after giving birth to our son, I began to get sick. I started swelling, having chest pains, shortness of breath, and couldn't walk far without getting tired. I felt as if an elephant was standing on my chest. I called my aunt who is a nurse and told her my symptoms and she quickly told me that I needed to go to the emergency room. I called the "ask a nurse" line and told them about my symptoms, they suggested that I immediately go to emergency room. I ignored what I was told and I kept saying I'll go later after I get some rest.

After my husband came home from work, I shared with him what was going on. He immediately took me to the emergency room. My parents came over to babysit our children so we wouldn't have to take them to the hospital with us. Once I was checked into the emergency room, the doctors began to run tests and labs to see what was going on with me. They were asking all kinds of questions and one question that stood out to me the most was, "Do you have aids?" I started thinking about the number of guys that I had had sex with. I begin to question myself. Fear begin to kick in and I thought I was about to die. My husband was there by my side the whole time. I could see the alarm and apprehension in his eyes. He was trying his best to stay strong for me; he didn't want me to worry.

The nurse came into the room and she told me my blood was clotted, I thought what is really going on? As time passed by that night, the doctors revealed what was going on with me. They discovered that I had Peripartum Cardiomyopathy (PPCM). PPCM is an uncommon disorder associated with pregnancy in which the heart dilates and weakens, leading to symptoms of heart failure. This explained where my symptoms were coming from. At the time, I didn't understand the severity of the diagnosis when my doctor explained it to me and I continued to get worse as time passed. The second day, I remember the doctors coming in my room asking me all kinds of questions about a will and my children. The doctor stated that I should have my family bring my children to the hospital so that I could spend as much time with them as I possibly could.

I knew then it was time to get my life right, I felt as if my sickness wasn't unto death. The doctors weren't expecting me to make it, but didn't know how long I had left on earth. There was something on the inside that kept telling me I shall live and not die—God had a plan for my life. Before all of this took place, I wasn't attending anyone's church, let alone, had a relationship with God. I was afraid of dying, I was a newlywed, had a newborn, and three other children that needed me as well as me needing them. I didn't want my children to have to be raised without their mother. Someway, somehow, I was determined and praying to overcome the sickness. That same day in the hospital, I had visits from family and friends. Nurses were coming into my room to take my vitals and they would ask what I was doing on that floor; that floor wasn't for me. At that time, I was the youngest patient on the heart floor.

Through it all, my husband stuck by my side, he was an awesome nurse. My hospital room soon flooded with family and friends coming to see and pray for me. The doctors continued to give me medicine to help with the pain and the other symptoms. There was a nurse who came to pick me up from my room to take me to try to walk. As she, my husband, and myself left my room and family, she said, "Why are you here? You are too young to be on this floor. We will not receive the report that the doctor has given you. You have some work to do; God isn't done with you yet." I didn't understand what she was telling me at the time, she told me when she came back to work two days later that she better not see me on that floor or in the hospital. The doctors continued to monitor me and run tests; they were waiting to see if I would improve. At the time, they had done all that they could do and made sure I was comfortable. I remember laying in the hospital bed after everyone had left one night. I began to pray and asked God to come see about a sinner such as myself. I wasn't sure if God was listening because it had been such a long time since he had heard from me.

I was discharged from the hospital after a few days. I guess God did hear little old me. I had several medications that I had to take and was placed under a doctor's care for about a year and a half. I promised to obey the doctor's orders as well as do what I had to do to get better. Every doctor's appointment, my doctors were amazed at my speedy recovery. They explained the seriousness of my sickness and that they really didn't expect me to recover. To God be the glory for his healing power! After a year, I was pretty much back to normal. It was time for me to get my life together and start a new life. God had showed me that he hears a sinner's prayer and He is a God of a second chance. I just wanted my life to be back to normal and to be able to take care of my family. My health started improving and I was able to do my normal routines. Six months had passed and I was about to graduate from ATC, which was another sign of God being with me. I felt like I had finally accomplished one of my goals in life.

A few months later God had completely healed my body. I didn't have to take any more medicine. I had graduated, I was working, taking care of my family, going to church and doing everything that I could. I was in a place of gratefulness—I was grateful to God for blessing me with another chance at life. My husband was supportive of me and often saw things in me that I didn't see in myself. My husband would always encourage me to go further and not to settle for less. One day my husband gave me some information for this university to pursue a bachelor's degree, I was hesitant about researching the school. He told me I could do whatever I put my mind to; he believed in me the most when I didn't believe in myself the least.

I decided to research the university to see if this would be of interest to me. I wanted to attend, but I felt as if I wasn't smart enough to pursue a bachelor's degree. My husband would constantly encourage me to enroll and not to let fear and doubt hold me back. I decided to take him up on his offer, he told me he would help me in any way that he could. I enrolled into the university and a short time later, I was surprised to hear that I had been accepted and I could pursue my degree. I prayed and asked God to lead and guide me along this journey; I didn't know how I was going to make it. I was the first in my family to pursue a secondary degree; most of my family had only a high school diploma. The journey was rough at times but I was determined to make it. I knew if God had healed me from heart problems, he would definitely help me through school. I had an awesome support system and my family was there with me along the way as well as praying with and for me.

There were times when my parents would come over to visit and I would be writing a paper, cooking, doing laundry, and taking care of my children. My husband would be at work or just getting home. My children would be playing around or watching television and making a lot of noise and dad would tell me he didn't see how I could get my homework done with the distractions. I would smile and tell dad that I heard them but I didn't hear them; I was accustomed to the noise. I was able to manage everything that I had going on. I'd learned from being a single parent that I had to do what I had to do regardless of who was there or not to help me. So this journey that I was on at the time wasn't any different from what I had going on when I was determined to be successful as a single parent. To God be the glory, after a few years, and even with the distractions, I graduated with my bachelor's. It was a wonderful feeling. I felt as if God had taken everything negative that I experienced in my past and turned it around for my good.

Now that I had my degree, my husband and some of my family encouraged me to pursue yet another degree. I didn't think I could do it. I thought it would be more work and harder than the bachelor's degree. By the help of the Lord, I decided to pursue my master's. People began to wonder how I was able to juggle life and further my education. As long as I kept God first and had a support system, there was nothing in this life that I felt I couldn't do. When God is in it, the sky is the limit. God guided me through the master's program within a year and a half. I was an example to my family and others of what God can do as long as you put him first and trust him with your life.

Twelve Years Later

You're tired and drained, got rid
of the pain.
You've done all you knew to do all of
these years.
You've worked hard, you've worked
doubles, went to school full time
and came home and did a mother's job.
Girl, you've done it all by yourself
without his help or support
Now, your life has paid off for all
your hard work
You finally found the man who loves
ya'll and bends over backwards for
his family
Life is good!
Here comes Donor out of nowhere,
decides he wants a paternity test
Your mind is telling you to say and
do things, but girl, that's not you.
Just shake it off and know that
God got this.
It was God's grace and mercy
that kept and brought you this far.
Why and what made Donor decide
to get a paternity test? Who knows, it's not
going to make a difference.

Chapter 6

Some may wonder how I made it through everything that I went through and still continue to smile. After God gave me a second chance in life and showing me that he got me, I had no choice but to push forward in life and overcome my circumstances. In the fall of 2006, I went to church with my brother Greg, Jr. for revival. The preacher preached a message that convicted my heart and penetrated in my soul. After service was over, my brother began to witness to me about God and salvation and he asked if I wanted to be baptized in Jesus' name. At the time, I didn't fully understand, but I knew I wanted to do whatever I had to do to show God how much I loved and appreciated him. I told my brother that I wanted to get baptized so he told me we would go back to church that Friday night so that I could get baptized. Friday night came and I was nervous but ready, I went down in Jesus name and I came out of the water feeling like a new person. I had the feeling my life was starting over again and this time I had to do right. I had to get past the negative thoughts that I had against church.

God was dealing with me about church. I was raised up in the church, but turned away from it and God. Seeing and experiencing different things in the church when I was younger caused me to leave the church once I was old enough and out of my parent's home. I was at a place in my life where I knew I needed God and I needed to be in church. I had to let go of those things that were hindering me from God, even the thoughts I had against the church. I visited various churches trying to find my way, but each church I visited didn't give me the peace that I needed to let me know I was in the right place.

I was invited to visit Redeem Tabernacle Church of Our Lord Jesus Christ. As soon as I walked in I immediately felt like that was going to be my church. I didn't tell anyone that

I was thinking this was the church for my family and I. One Sunday my husband was able to go to church with us and we happened to have a great service that Sunday. Later that night, my husband and I were talking and he said, "Baby, I enjoyed church today, I want that to be our family church." I told him that I had the same thought and we should join. I was a little hesitant because I was thinking about all of the things that had been said about what we couldn't do because it seemed as if everything was a sin growing up.

After attending several services at Redeem, we eventually took the right hand of fellowship and joined the church. My desire to learn and to know God grew stronger each day. It was finally time to get my spiritual life lined up with my natural life. I felt like I was a baby in God because I didn't know him although he knew and loved me. My faith continued to grow daily and my love for God was even greater. During the summer of July 2007, I went to the International Holy Convocation in Columbia, South Carolina. There were people from all over the world, all in one place. God began to deal with me and I was determined not to leave the convocation the same way that I came. During the midday service on that Saturday, I received my breakthrough, I received the gift of the Holy Ghost, speaking other tongues as the spirit gives utterance. God was just blessing me over and over again.

The love that the church members showed and shared with my family was unbelievable. In the beginning, I thought it was too good to be true; there was no way anyone could have that much love for someone. The love that they showed continues to show today even greater as well as the support. There is something special about each and every one of my church family that I look forward to seeing. They have been instrumental in my life as well as my family life.

I often look back over my life and realize where God has pulled me from. In the midst of my sins and imperfections, God continues to show me grace and mercy. Through everything that I went through, the negative thoughts and comments continue to hunt me. I was told repeatedly by friends, family, and men I thought loved me that I would never amount to anything; no one would ever want me; there was no way I could go to college when I had children to raise; I would never get married; I was going to keep having children by different men; I would never finish school; I would be on government assistance; my children would never be anything; the list is long. People tried to make me feel as if I was the only one who ever sinned and people immediately judged me by my situation.

The hurt I had to deal with was from friends but more so from my family. My family hurt me the most; the people who I thought would be there for me. When no one else was there for me or to support me, I expected my family to be. The trials and tribulations that I went through with family and friends is what pushed me so hard to make it in this world. Yes, I had lived a sinful life, but that didn't give anyone reason to judge or crucify me. Everything positive that I did or tried to do, the more people tried to break me down. I was determined to be the opposite of what everyone had said about me.

People thought my marriage wasn't going to last because my husband and I met in a club. Supposedly, people who meet in a club aren't meant to last forever or in a relationship period. Who is to say? There were times when I thought our marriage wouldn't work and we weren't going to last. Marriage is a commitment that I take seriously, though. Even when I was younger, I knew marriage was supposed to be sacred. Regardless of everything that we've been through in our marriage, we have been strong together.

My husband has been the husband that I would've never thought I would have. In the earlier part of our marriage, well a month and half into our marriage, he proved that we would be together through sickness and health. he was there throughout my season of sickness; someone else probably would've left me to go through it alone. God used my husband in many ways to encourage me through everything.

With my husband's love and support, my children and I are able to pursue or goals. He constantly tells us he work as hard as he can just so that we can live out our dreams. Although he can't make it to everything, we participate in or events that we have, he makes sure we have what we need. I appreciate and love him so much, just for being the man that he is. He sacrifices so much for our family. I wouldn't be half the woman that I am today if I didn't allow God to use him to be who he needed to be in our life. When people said I would never get married or no one would want me with children by different men, God sent me a husband who not only loves me, but loves my children as his own. Throughout the years when their biological daddies wouldn't be bothered to be involved in my children's live or pay child support, my husband would tell me not to worry about it. He would say that our children would be taken care of regardless of whether or not I received child support for them. As I look back over my life, there was so much hurt and pain that made me want to give up but God gave me strength to endure everything that I encountered. Growing up sheltered and living the life that I did, I never imagined my life would be like this. People tried their best to tear me down along the way. People, who said they had my back and would be here for me, were the ones who used me. People said I would never be or have anything, but God proved them wrong.

All of the negative talk about no one would ever want me, a girl with children by different men, God blessed me with a husband who loves my children and I.

People said I would be on welfare; today I work a full time job and we're not eligible to receive any government assistance.

I was told I'd never graduate. Well, I graduated from high school and have a bachelor's and master's degree.

I was told the Lord would never bless me for having children out of wedlock, or bless my children, but today my household is blessed and a living testimony.

People said I would just run the streets and be clubbing all my life. I'm now running the streets for Jesus and churching for the rest of my life.

The people that I thought I was losing, God showed me that I didn't lose anything. I gained more and better of what I thought I had.

Don't ever accept the things that people say that tries to tear you down or keep you from being who God intended for you to be. A person tends to speak things about other people because that's how they truly feel about themselves. Stop worrying about what people think or what people are going to say, at the end of the day, how is that benefiting you or anything in your life? Don't focus on what that person is thinking or saying; you will miss out on so much worrying about something that doesn't even matter. Had I listened to all of those naysayers, I wouldn't be who I am today. Yes, it did hurt and bother me during that time but it didn't stop me. Everyone falls short of the glory—everyone goes through things and we all make mistakes. People pretend that they have it all together, but if walls could talk, we would see people for who they really are.

Whenever God is blessing you and taking you to another level, those same people who have so much to say will eventually fall away. Some people can't handle the way God blesses you. It is during that time when God is getting ready to elevate you; he shows you the truth of the person and how they really feel about you. Don't worry about "people"; their opinion is their opinion. However, God is going to bless you and equip you, you're going to do just that regardless of what they think. God does not ask someone who knows you if he can bless you or do anything for you, he does it because he is God. So why should we worry about the negative comments, thoughts and actions from people.

God had to move some people out of my life so that he could place the people that needed to be in my life. Don't worry about the people who turn their back on you, just thank God in advance that they're turning their back so that you can move forward. Anytime you're facing the back of something or someone, you can't move forward. God doesn't take things from us so that we could be without; he takes things out of our life so that he can bless us with the things that are greater than what we could ask for or think of.

To the people who said I wouldn't be blessed because I had children out of wedlock: God is using my children to be a blessing to me. According to some people, my children were going to be a curse and I was going to have to keep bailing them out of trouble. Thank God, people don't have the last say so over my life and children. My children are the opposite of what people said or thought they would be. My oldest son is spreading God's word as well as living it; he is allowing God to use him in a mighty way. God has anointed and appointed him to continue the work of the Lord and draw others to Christ.

My daughter, whom I was going to abort, is full of life. She brightens the room when she enters and she brings life and smiles to any and every one. My daughter has a beautiful voice to sing. God has given her a gift that he's going to edify to be a blessing and encourager to others. Although she's small in size, she has a heart the size of the world to do what she can for any and every one. She's my only daughter and she's such a blessing. I often stare at her and give God thanks for not allowing me to abort such a gift. When God has birthed something inside of us, something that we're going to use for his glory, we tend to abort the blessing that's going to change our lives. What was intended to be me my abortion, God birthed to be my deliverer.

My son, my third baby is growing and changing others' lives as well. He has a heart for people and is willing to help those who are in need or are lacking. God has placed a gift in him that makes him unique. We often call Eric our "ball boy"; ever since he started walking, he's always carried a basketball wherever he goes. He can write using both hands as well as play basketball with either hand. He has a heart to help the less fortune, and although he may not say much about what he sees, he'd rather step up and make a difference. He often tells my husband and I that when he grows up, he's going to move us in with him. He has witnessed our sacrifices and struggles and constantly says how much he love and appreciate us. There are times when you're doing all that you know to do and have no choice but to push harder, you never know who's watching you. God can take the same person who's watching your life and use them to bless and deliver you out of your struggle.

My youngest son loves sports, we often call him my "dark child" because he has the darkest skin out of all my children. When the doctor had said I would never have children, God joined my husband and I together to boost our lightness. We were in darkness and God used the birth of my son to bring us to the light. My son loves sports and loves people. He is always willing to help children who are younger than him. He's our protector; whenever his dad isn't home, although he's the youngest, he tries to protect everyone. He has his unique way of sharing his heart and showing us love. When you think God has closed your womb from conceiving a child, just know He's never done.

Just when I thought God had closed my womb, he opened it up and conceived me with the birth of this book. Pregnancy doesn't always mean you're pregnant with a human being; you could be pregnant with potential, life, healing, deliverance, success, education, promotions and so on. Ask yourself "What am I pregnant with, what am I about to birth?"

My children are my blessings, people tried to make me feel as if they were my punishment. God is a forgiving God, God allows us to go through things just so that we can help the next person along his or her journey. Everything that I have been through in my past was not for me but for those who was lost such as myself. Although I have four children by different men, there's one man who restores everything together to get one happy family under the same roof. Regardless of how many children and baby daddies you may have, God can restore everything that you once lost. God can heal your heart, deliver you out of an abusive relationship, physically and verbally, send you love as well as show you how to love and trust again. When you think your life is over or you want to throw in the towel, pray and trust God to work it all out. The only thing that can hold you back from being who God wants you to be is you. People don't have the final say or any say at all over your life. Let the negative words from people flow off of your mind like the water flows off of a ducks back.

Never settle for less. When people say you can't, God says you can. God is waiting for us to reach out to him so he can deliver us out of our situations. The times when I thought I was alone and God was further away from me, he was right beside me the whole time. God is only going to do what we allow him to do in our lives. All God wants to know is how bad do we want it and how bad do we need him. You don't have to be a bible scholar or holier than thou for God to hear you and answer your prayers. I was a sinner with a lost soul, who needed to be found and delivered. Even after I got saved, I had people who tried to continue to beat me down. There were some people in the church who tried to make me feel like I wasn't worthy or God wasn't going to forgive me. The love of God that abides in me helps me to forgive those people and continue to pray for them.

I am somebody, I am worthy, forgiving, restored, delivered, healed, loved and a woman of God, what anyone else thinks or feels has no benefit in my life. For years, I hid so much behind my smile but God came in and gave me a pure smile. I was supposed to be broken and lost but God said not so. Live your life and trust God; let God be the reason behind your smile.

God has restored and blessed me with a wonderful life. I'm finally free, confident and letting God take the wheel over my life. People didn't want to see me rise above my past and situations, whenever God blessed me, someone would say, "you remember how you use to sneak guys into your parents' house" or "you remember when you and your husband was going to separate." Someone is always looking to throw a stone in the way of your breakthrough. In life we have to take those same stones to build a hill to climb out of whatever we're going through. Whenever God bless you, there will always be someone to remind you of what you did in the past. They want to remember you for what you did or who you were in the past instead of remembering where you're going in the future.

I received various "no" and rejections in my past. I've experienced not being qualified for government assistance at times, I didn't receive child support, certain jobs I wasn't eligible for, but I was determined to keep pushing and not letting any of that detour me from where I was trying to go or what I was trying to do. Even in the midst of it all, God was still looking out for me and making a way out of no way. God was there with me along this journey called life and he looked passed all of my flaws and blessed me over and over again. People called me all kinds of names in my past, they even lied to me, but this happened to Jesus as well. That is why I'm here today. Jesus experienced everything that I went through and that's how he knew to lead and guide me to this place in life.

I've learned people judge you because of where you are or what you've done because they haven't walked in your shoes. It's easy to say what someone should or shouldn't do or what you would or would've done if it was you. A person may never know how he or she may react to a certain situation until they have crossed the bridge that you crossed over. It's the same way in church — we're so quick to judge those who have sin or sinning and forget that we all have sinned. No one was created to be perfect but Jesus Christ himself. If we were perfect, we would've never needed a savior. Instead of looking and judging someone, what are we going to do to help our brother or sister out of their situation or sin? We can talk about them all day and night but that's not helping them at all. We have to remember that someone did or said something that caused us to get out of the sin that we were once in. When we see our brother or sister falling, let's be strong enough and be in a place ourselves so that we may help them up. The same person that we're judging and gossiping about, that could be us. When we see someone making mistakes, sinning or don't have it together, ask yourself "what can I do to help this person instead of wasting my energy judging and talking about the individual?" Remember everyone has done something that wasn't pleasing to God, some of us hide it, but if the covers were to be pulled back, we would see that we're in no better shape than the person we're crucifying.

Just because someone is smiling, that doesn't mean that everything is okay. The smile is a sign of being in need of something, for years I hid behind my smile and no one knew my tears that I shed at night. I hid behind my smile and no one knew the pain that I was in. Look beyond your smile, look beyond someone else smile and see what it is that they're in need of or crying out for. Ask yourself "what's behind my smile?"

Epilogue

My Story Reveals God's Glory

You see, my story was written by an author by the name of Jesus Christ, but I plagiarized his story and wrote it the way I wanted it to go. I had everything all planned out and I just knew I was going to be living the good life. So I thought,

My story went like this:

It was during my high school years and instead of enjoying my teenage years and high school, I was listening to the boys telling me everything I wanted to hear, I was under a lot of pressure from my peers, and I wanted to fit in. The consequences of doing those things led me to the story of a young teenage mother. I had my first child at sixteen, second at eighteen, third at twenty and fourth at twenty-four. After having my first child, I heard all kinds of negative talk spoken over my child and my life. People including family and friends said I was going to be another girl on welfare, I would never finish high school and become anyone, no man would want me, my child would be a troublemaker, and the list goes on. Those that said they would be there for me and have my back, they were the main ones trying to hinder me from becoming a success story, and they lied, took advantage of me, and pretended to be supportive. Some may ask if that bothered or offended me in any kind of way; of course it did. How many of you know that when people say the same thing over and over again about you whether it's true or not, you begin to believe what they're saying is true? I listened to them for a while, but I decided I wanted to be different than what they were about or calling me. The more they tried to tear me down, the harder I worked to prove them wrong,

I graduated from high school with two children, just so you'll understand where I'm coming from. My daughter is in the tenth grade and I had my first child in the tenth grade. My oldest son is a senior in high school. At his age, I was getting ready to walk across the stage with a big belly and not a belly stuffed with food, but with my second child. To God be the glory, neither one of my children have any or are expecting any babies in their high school years. See, people told me my children would repeat my past and it's just going to continue from generation to generation. If I had let people write my story, I wouldn't be standing here today. There were so many stumbling blocks along the way but I knew it was only a setup for my comeback. Those same people are wondering today how I started out so wrong but ended up on the right path. Some wonder why I didn't give up, why I didn't just turn my back and walk away. I am a survivor, I am an over comer, I am victorious, I am saved and wonderfully made, I know who I am and who I belong to, I know who wrote my story (the author and finisher of my life), and that is why I serve no other God but Jesus Christ.

My story can go on and on about how I got to where I am today. Some of you wouldn't believe the things I went through and dealt with if I were to tell you. Once I stopped listening to the negative stuff, and started believing in God, I turned the pen over to him and let him finish writing my story. Once I repented, got baptized in Jesus' name and received the gift of the Holy Ghost, everything else just started lining up. Those stumbling blocks, the hurt and pain that were in my way were put in my path to help me get to where God was trying to lead me. I didn't want that life at that time; I thought living the life God had planned for me would be boring, especially listening to the saints teach and preach about you can't do this, you can't do that, you can't go here or you can't go there. I finally got the chance to experience the prom life at the age of thirty-two (that's another story). Well, at the age of thirty-three, I see God's plan is not boring. Sometimes God allows us to take the wrong path so once we find and trust him, we will stay on the right path.

Don't let anyone write your story. Don't let the stumbling blocks block out the author and finisher of your life. Teenagers, it is not all what your peers say it is or what you think it is. It's not worth the pressure; let God reveal your story to them so that he can get the glory and watch how you would be pressuring them by the life you live. Take it from someone who has been on the same path that you're on; I thought I was living the good life. The day of graduation, walk across that stage with empty bellies ladies, and your pants pulled up young men, and trust God with the story of your life. He's the number one author in my life. The story of my life reveals God's glory; what does your story reveal?

It's Behind Her Smile

In Memorium

My Angel
Inez McGee Givens (August 29 1940-April 2, 2010)

Grandma,

I miss you so much. Words can't express the way my heart feels and wishing you were still here. I have had some grieving nights wishing I could call you and just share with you everything that is going on. I miss our conversations and laughs and seeing your pretty, bright smile. Grandma, when no one else understood me, you always understood and encouraged me to move pass the situations. You were the only one who I could come to and talk to about any and everything. You knew and understood where I was coming from. We shared the same situations from dead-end relationships to having children out of wedlock by different men. I remember how much you use to always tell me to write my books and although I was afraid, you were excited for me as if it had already came to past. Grandma, you believed in me when I didn't believe in myself. You prayed with and for me and you always knew when and how to encourage me. People, including family, would always judge me and say I wouldn't amount to anything. You taught me how to be strong and not let what others say about me stop from becoming successful and the woman who God made me to be. The prayer that my grandmother prayed has been answered. You were always a praying woman of God and your faith encouraged me to have faith and trust God all the way.

Grandma, this book is in memory of you. You witnessed everything that I encountered along the way. There are some things that you even carried to your grave, only God knows. While writing this book, there were some moments that were hard for me, but God guided me through it. I know you would be proud of me right now and if no one else rejoiced with me, you would. I thank God for having a praying grandmother and you prayed for little old me.

My Angel

Grandma, I miss you so much,
If I only could get one more chance to feel your touch.
Although I feel you left us too soon,
God knew best and called you home in His heavenly room.
Our conversations we shared, the tears we shed, the smiles, the laughs,
The struggles, the pain, but most definitely, everything that we gained.
You knew and prayed that this day would come,
Oh how I hear you saying "Baby, well done".
When no one else knew what I was dealing with
You were there to encourage and pray me through.
Although you're not here to witness this day,
I know your prayers led me this way.
My angel,
Smile now and spread your wings,
Writing a book has always been my dream.
Now that you're gone,
Memories of you continue to live on.
My angel, my heart;
Writing this book was just the start.

About the Author

LaTasha S. Woodcock was born and raised in Augusta, Georgia. She is the only daughter and oldest child of three of George and Patricia Gore. LaTasha resides in Hephzibah, Georgia, with her husband, Howard, and four children Marquis, Ny'Zeria, Eric, and Denzil. LaTasha has a unique way of encouraging, inspiring, motivating, and serving others. Her smile lights up those around her wherever she goes. LaTasha is always willing to help others overcome whatever life has presented.

We tend to look at people and their current situation and we immediately begin to judge. Instead of offering and lending a hand or uplifting the individual, we tear them down even further. We have so much to say about other individuals but ignore what's in front of us in the mirror. We never know what someone may be going through or dealing with behind their smile.

> "When they said I couldn't, I took a front row seat to watch their reactions when God showed them He could."
>
> – LaTasha S. Woodcock

LaTasha S. Woodcock

Author LaTasha Woodcock's smile does not mean that everything in her life is perfect. Her smile is to hide what she's really dealing with on the inside — it's her comfort zone. Seeking to fill a void in her life led her to depend on men to make her feel happy and loved. Longing for a relationship, attention, and love from her family led her to seek it from people who weren't good for her. Throughout her journey, she dealt with betrayal, abuse, cheating, and abandonment.

As a single mom of three, she often had to work double shifts, clean toilets, stock coolers or whatever was asked of her, just to make sure my children were taken care of. Being a single parent and having to play the role of both parents was a challenge, but she was determined not to be another statistic. When people said that she would never amount to anything and no one would ever want her, God had the final say.